CW00971982

LOVE
and
BEING
LOVED

LOVE
and
BEING
LOVED

Love Letters and Original Love Poems

LEW

XULON PRESS

Xulon Press
2301 Lucien Way #415
Maitland, FL 32751
407.339.4217
www.xulonpress.com

© 2022 by LEW

Contribution by: Joyita Sanchez

All rights reserved solely by the author. The author guarantees all contents are original and do not infringe upon the legal rights of any other person or work. No part of this book may be reproduced in any form without the permission of the author.

Due to the changing nature of the Internet, if there are any web addresses, links, or URLs included in this manuscript, these may have been altered and may no longer be accessible. The views and opinions shared in this book belong solely to the author and do not necessarily reflect those of the publisher. The publisher therefore disclaims responsibility for the views or opinions expressed within the work.

Paperback ISBN-13: 978-1-66286-450-6
Ebook ISBN-13: 978-1-66286-451-3

Introduction

THIS IS THE story of two people in love that live and work in different countries. Portrayed within is how true love can work with open communication. If you love someone you need to let them know, expressing how special their love is to you. Communication, honesty, respect, loyalty and friendship build a relationship foundation. Notice and compliment your partner's thoughtfulness and sensitivities. Little annoyances should not scare love away. A bad temper has no place in a love relationship. Be the best at all these things, and your mate will return your love.

Within these pages are expressive text messages, letters, and original poems. I assembled it for people to gain ideas to write their own texts or letters, or borrow some phrases for special occasions. Begin reading and explore the many facets of love.

Dear Luke,

Every time I see the sun die behind the mountains and the arrival of night covers me in its dark cloak, I will remember your face, fragile and strong, showing love. The darkness will shine in the immortal splendor of your smile. At that moment, I will hear your voice carried by the wind, which will whisper softly, "I love you," and an invisible hand will touch my face in a caress. Then I will understand that when you left, you did not abandon me. I can't see you, but I know you are there! You are here by my side, guiding and protecting me. With this certainty that calms my wounded heart, one and a thousand times more I will tell you, "Love, I love you, too! I will love you forever, for life . . . and beyond!"

I wish to see, in time, the desire to love and to be loved, to chase that star that lights up life, to believe in the memory of a lost love, to bravely continue the fight in the infinite darkness. A drowsiness envelopes the body, a memory emerges to the mind, a fire before going out that slowly, slowly ignites again. I have a wish to hide in that wonderful smile of yours. Let me discover that new world that smiles in your eyes, a new world with all the colors of the rainbow, a new world that forms the first steps and shows me who I can trust to savor life. All I ask of you is a dream, a dream that transports us from the sky to the sea, like the sun that rises every dawn—a dream of infinite love, a dream that takes us far. Hide my love in your arms, put your mouth on mine, and we will travel through all the love in the world. Just for tonight let me rest in your huge eyes because I can't love you more (than that).

Joyita

Dear Joyita,

As one who has struck it rich in the conquest of love, I bear witness to the fact that it is very worthwhile to take a chance on love, if you and I are an example! I still cannot believe that you are not a dream! But you are better than a dream, with your sweetness and loving nature. You are like a song on the wind that just keeps my heart racing. You are the warmth and brightness of the sun, and your eyes sparkle like diamonds! When I look at the stars in the night sky, my heart races, thinking you are looking at the same night sky. I am wishing we were doing it together! Maybe I am in hell because I can only dream about you but not be with you. It may be punishment for past sins. I only hope the Lord has mercy, and we can be together in the future and stop this torture! Then again, living with me might be torture for you! Ha ha!

Yours,
Luke

Hi Luke,

Good afternoon. I hope that in this beautiful afternoon you find yourself in the best way. This time I am writing you this letter because from what I see, you do not want to share the messages with me. I know it may sound like I am an intense woman, but I am not. I'm just putting all my attention on you so that I can see you online, and you don't want to talk to me. I want you to know that I am really dying to get to know you more every day, and this feeling is growing. So if it's not too much to ask, I hope you can give me an answer because you have me worried.

And, I chose you because I realized that you can easily find my weak point, and you are the only one capable of discovering the way to calm this undeniable soul. I chose you because I realized that a life by your side would be worth much; it was worth the risks, it was worth trying to believe in love and in a new opportunity to be happy. I am not going to shut up what I feel for you; my feelings are pure and sincere and only seek to be captured in the depths of your heart. I want you to know that I want you to fall in love with me and become your reason for living. I want to be the reason why you wake up every morning happy and with a beautiful smile on your face. You deserve to be happy, and I want to be the one who can bring you that happiness.

Joyita

Jonita,

If I could give you one thing in life, I would give you the ability to see yourself through my eyes. Only then would you realize how special you are to me! I wanted to talk to you about something. I was thinking that we could live in my apartment for a short time until you get established with your job, and then we can decide not only what area we want to live but find a small farm that we both like. The good thing is if we find something and it is not perfect, I can change some things about it to make it perfect. I can do carpentry, plumbing, and electrical work, which will come in handy.

Love, Luke

Dear Luke,

From the very beginning of our communication, I was able to appreciate in you affection and sensitivity, amazing care, sincerity, and kindness. You know I can only find the most pleasant and positive character traits in you, which constantly confirm that I can be happiest with you. I am grateful to fate for meeting the best guy who is my soulmate, who is able to truly understand and provide worthy support in any life situation. I live with you alone and breathe. I always worship you and want to be together forever. I believe that our relationship will only get stronger, and we will be able to live our whole lives together, delighting each other every day, discovering new facets and understanding how wonderful our amazing relationship can be.

Joyita

Dear Luke,

I hope that you will understand everything that I want to tell you in this letter!

It is so strange and at the same time pleasant when, waking up in the morning and falling asleep at night, I miss you so much. I will follow you into the fire and into the water, and I will catch your every breath, every smile with all my heart, because I value you very much! I am ready to give you happiness! I can do it because you are my happiness! I believe in you, I believe in your strength, and I know that no matter what, I will be there for you! You know, it's so weird when you're not around. The feeling of separation is stronger than me because it is slowly killing me, depriving me of sleep and joy. The romance that you give me lifts me to heaven where I want to stay with you forever! If it were in my power, I would give you the universe; I would give you the sky, the moon and the sun. It would be so romantic, and you would be so romantic, and you would understand how much I need you. There are such feelings only once in a lifetime.

What do you think about my words?

Joyita

Dear Luke,

My heart felt faded like my old blue jeans until you came along and started it beating again. You made me see how blue the color of the sky is again. I now am more aware of how pretty the spring flowers are! I now hear the lovely songs of the cardinals, the robins, and other spring birds. You have made my whole life so much better with the love that you send me and me only. It is like I was a zombie, and now you have brought me back to life to really live and enjoy it. And you are the one and only that I want to enjoy it with, the only person that I want to spend the rest of my life with to enjoy and grow together. I love you more than I can say with manmade words, but I will show you how I love you every day and night of my life!

Joyita

Dear Luke,

You deserve someone who does not tell you how handsome you are but teaches you, so you can learn it without having to repeat it. You deserve a poem without adornment, direct phrases, plain and simple words, so that you understand that in love or poetry, it is what comes out of your mouth and not what you read in books. You deserve a love with a pure heart so that you know how to understand sadness when there are problems. But above all, I want to protect the damage to your heart.

Joyita

Dear Luke,

    I do not want to be the love of your life. I want to be the complement of your days, the companion of your twilight, and your friend of nostalgic sunsets. I want to be the owner of your dreams, who walks in the same direction and always at the same time. I want to travel toward the horizon of tomorrow; that is, I am the one who wants to teach you the most beautiful way to express the beautiful way of what it is to love.

    If you love me, then do not stray any further from me because lately you are becoming a habit to leave little by little from my side and collide as if nothing had happened, I would like to call out to you, and I will do it if necessary. Perhaps my words will not be received because you are immersed in other loves or hearts, and my love cannot reach you, but I hope that it can change and that my words will not be ignored.

Joyita

Dear Luke,

I never thought about getting what I am feeling now because I have seen so many fail in love, which made me decide not to take the risk to get hurt. However, all that changed when I met you because without wanting and without thinking, you came in to my life, and you ended up robbing me of my heart!

You fill my world with joy! I tend to feel my skin tingle, you make my hands swell, and my lips are not able to hide a magnificent smile, which only makes me understand that I have fallen in love with you.

Joyita

Love,

Yesterday no longer exists, and the future has not yet been born, so it is today that we have the opportunity to do things differently. To fight much more for the things we really want is not just another day.

Always ready to confess her love, putting only the best feeling into the spoken words. Dear, you allowed me to believe love exists!

Joyita

Dear Luke,

This is a brand new and beautiful day that begins, and we must make the most of it! So my dear, save these beautiful words, and let's change the way we see things from day to day. Let's fight for our love and not let anyone interrupt us. Instead, we will think about the beautiful future that awaits us. I want this to be a day full of much love and affection for our relationship. I want us to have a happy day, filled with many good things for our future life together. Do not forget that I love you with all my being. I send you many kisses for those beautiful lips of yours.

Joyita

Dear Joyita,

You are not only a beautiful, intelligent, and caring person, but you have accomplished so much in your young life. Being a doctor took determination, hard work, and sacrifice of your free time to study. You had to be focused and smart to remember everything you needed to learn that profession. I see in you that little girl that you keep inside you and hope you never lose that as it is a beautiful part of you. If I really told you how I felt about you, I would have to make a list. There is so much to you as a person that it cannot be explained in a few words.

I am so flattered that you contacted me. But I want to make sure your understand that I am seventy-two years old and still healthy and strong, but as a doctor you know that will change over the years. Of course, I could be thirty years old and killed by a car tomorrow. I just see the treasure within you that other men have missed! They must just be looking for trophies, not a great partner. I don't want a slave (I know how to do laundry), but an equal partner whom I will teach what real love is, as I have a big heart.

Luke

Luke,

Yes, I really know the work I have done has been quite hard, but it has been worth it. I already told you, really, age is not what interests me about you; what really interests me about you, what really interests me, is being able to be there for you and what you need the most. I told you that I would be the woman who would help you with your health.

Jonita

Joyita,

The truth is that I would like to spend more time with you since you are really a person worth fighting for, and when I say that, it is because it is really worth it. You are a wonderful person and I really like you. Well, I really like you also, but asking you to leave friends and family to go to a strange country and language is asking a lot. You are well established there also, with your work. I would never want to stress you as it is not in my personality. If we do become one, then we would vacation there to visit family and friends, but again, I do not want to stress you in any way. You could easily get a good income here with your credentials, but it would be your money because you earn it. I am not rich but do okay, so I only want you and the beautiful person you are, not your money.

Luke

Dear Luke,

I write this letter to you since you have impressed me for being that great person that you are. You really leave me impressed by the quality of the person that you are. I really admire you for being that unconditional father to your children. You remind me how my grandfather was. What a warrior he was. You know you deserve the best of this world, and I would be the best for you. I would really like to continue knowing you and to have a good rhythm in our feelings. You have seemed a fantastic person to me. I hope you like this tasting and that you can give me an answer to such beautiful feelings that I left in this letter.

Joyita

Luke,

My beloved, as always thinking about my well-being and when I feel comfortable. Thanks for your love; you make me very happy every day. You always bring me a smile of affection, with your protection, your details, your love, your work, your support, your guidance and your effort you make for us every day. The truth is, I could continue listing the many beautiful things, my love, that you have brought to me, and I really want to tell you how I appreciate and love you for it. You taught me to smile constantly, and it is something that I have stayed so far from in the past. Thanks for keeping my heart happy. I hope to have a lot of time by your side. I will do everything possible so that every day you fall in love with me as a way to thank you for everything you do for me.

Joyita

Luke,

I cannot help but think of you every night, feeling you close with every moon, looking at the stars. Luke, darling, the distance does not kill this love because your smile is always on my mind and because your eyes continue to shine when I think of you!

It is only material things that drive us away, but nothing can silence this feeling; nothing can kill such passion. The more time passes and the more I love you, you become part of me. I feel you with every heartbeat, and I invoke you every second. I adore you with all my being. You are my great love, my support, and my relief in the distance. I love you madly.

Jozita

Joyita,

    I want to tell you everything I feel, when you speak to me and when I see you because I cannot shut up this beautiful feeling that you have put on me since the day I met you. I want to tell you that I am in love and that, without thinking, you ended up becoming my reason for living. You are that special reason I wake up every morning with a smile on my face and a great determination to go out and eat the world. That's why I write this letter of love and express my desire to be held by your side, to show you how much I love you and how happy I can be—if you decide one day to stay by my side.

                      Luke

My love,

Thank you for your response letter! I love you more than yesterday and tomorrow; when I wake up, I will love you more than today! I am ready to give you all my love every day, and from this, my love for you will constantly grow! I want to make your life better, give you what you lack, and make your every day happy! Are you ready to help me with this? I noticed that many people underestimate the power of words. I am sure that sincere conversation can solve many problems. It is the ability to speak from heart to heart that helps people maintain relationships for life!

I think heart-to-heart conversation is the key to maximum intimacy forever! We must open our hearts to each other, share the most valuable memories and thoughts, and then we can be together forever. I think a lot of people don't work on building an emotional connection when entering a relationship. That's why they can't be together for long. First, the chemistry keeps them together. Then they start to crash and break up. And they don't fix their relationship because they haven't become 100 percent special to each other. Let's open our hearts to each other and become the closest people in the world! Let our thoughts merge together, our hearts beat in unison, and

we will become the closest people in the entire universe!
I believe that this is possible only between us because I see
that our souls are similar and strive for each other! I want
to show you these photos and my passionate and hot videos! I
will wait for your opinion on my letter; will you answer me?

Jonita

Joyita,

As I have told you, I am totally in love with you. You are the dream woman I have always dreamed about but never found until now. You have sparked the feeling of love in heart that I had not felt in many, many years. I have had women try to make me fall in love, but you are the very first woman in a long time to do it. You have done it very well because before this, I would never even consider having something with a woman from another country, especially one so much younger than me. So it must be God because I feel it is something bigger than the two of us. One thing I must tell you is that I am very, very happy about it, and so I do not regret one moment that I spend with you. On the contrary, I love every moment we spend together and cannot wait to do it in person.

Love you always,
your Luke

Joyita,

How could I ever deserve such a woman as you are?
You not only speak the truth but speak it with feeling
and humility. You have knowledge beyond your years on
relationships and emotions. You are not only a dream to look
at but a pleasure to converse with. You are a true treasure,
and you bring immense happiness to my heart and mind. You
are the first and only person other than God to own my soul.
You have worked hard to gain your knowledge and skills to
help others who need your training. Yet you carry all that
is within you with kindness and do not act above others
by being arrogant or stuck up. You are not only a child of
God, but a follower of his teachings. My heart is so full
with love for you that it should split apart and spill out to
take up more space than all the world's oceans. I enjoy your
humor, and laughing with you is such a joy to me.
    It is like a dream I have since a child, to find a true
love that would be above all my expectations so that I would
get some of the things I hoped for. But like I would say
to you, you are the dream I hope I never wake up from. You
are so perfect in so many ways; that is why I gave you a
list that only brushes the surface of what is in my heart.
It is some of my feelings and things I love about you. So I

needed to write this short note to let you know part of what I feel and love about you!

Luke

Joyita,

In these uncertain times I sometimes ask myself what is real. And I have one thing that anchors me every time, and that is the way I feel. I feel as though we are two hearts born to love beating as one. And eventually we will be in heaven when you come. Now we are like two ships in the night passing each other in the seas, floating around hoping to find our destination when the sun comes up and be home. But rest assured, my destination is you. All you have to do is be strong, and we will get through these rough seas together. You know you make me light as a feather, so in this storm, we will brave together and be assured that there will be a place where your heart will be safe in the harbor of my heart. And when finally together, we will never part!

Love you!

Luke

Luke,

The moment I first saw you, you were standing in the middle of a crowd laughing and talking to a friend. There was something about you; maybe it was the way you laughed or the way your eyes lit up. But I knew this undeniable attraction was what I felt for you. I was shy, nervous, and a bit hesitant when I asked you to dance with me. We were strangers, and when you said yes, I swear my heart skipped a beat. Since that night I've known we were meant to be together. And not a day goes by that your love doesn't prove me right. I love you much more than you can imagine, and I just want you to stay mine forever.

Joyita

Joyita,

I missed you when I ran out of credits. I never could put how I really feel about you in to words because it would fill a book, but not being an author, that would be difficult for me. But since I met you at a distance, you have turned my world upside down. I now see and feel the work in beautiful colors because you brighten my day. You turn my nights bright with the beautiful and sweet words you say.

I was walking around previously in this world in the dark,

until I answered a message from a beautiful woman as a lark.

I feel like I am underwater because you take my breath away,

but it is all okay,

and I still have many words to say.

You make me light as a feather and I can't wait to be together.

My heart beats faster when we talk.

I can't wait for us to be under the stars together for a walk.

Luke

Hi Luke,

It would be nice to say that it is a pleasure if you could be for me and, of course, I'd like to know that I can have a bad boy. You know what I mean, because I can be proud to say that I'm leaving. I may be a stranger from your hands now, but I wish that we could travel the world without any doubt. For now I'm a model and want to get as high as possible, good and admirable, but with a lot of professionalism. I am constantly reading books, knowing more especially and not only being a pretty face, ha ha. I have and ask for a good sense of humor or something else, like the secret touch that you can put on, so just look at me and let an interesting moment happen. I send you hugs.

Joyita

Luke,

The next time I see you, I will cover you with love, with ecstasy. I will stuff you with all the joys of the flesh so that you faint and die of exhaustion.

I want you to marvel at me and to confess to yourself that you never even dreamed of being transported like that. When you are old, I want you to remember these few hours. I want your dry bones to tremble with joy when you think of it! May the world burn around us as I fill you with hugs, no matter how I do it. You are the best love.

Joyita

Luke,

I am crazy about you! I can't think of anything other than you anymore. Despite myself, my imagination leads me to think of you. I can't put two ideas together without you coming between them. I can't think of anything different from you anymore. Despite myself, my imagination leads me to think of you.

I grab you, I kiss you, I caress you, a thousand of the most loving caresses take me over. As for my heart, there you will be very present. I have a delicious feeling about you. But my God, what will become of me now that you have deprived me of reason? This is a mania that terrifies me this morning.

Joyita

Joyita,

I am thinking of the right words to say today to tell you how much I miss your smile. And then I must compile the words to let you know how your love makes me as a man grow and to do the things as a team to plant our love seeds. The seeds teach me to love and please you! I am always thinking to do more things that you like instead of things that are stinking (like working on cars), such as going with you on a mountain hike. I want to do something special like buy you flowers or purchase something to organize your hiking gear, like a satchel. But even though I love you so, and this you should know, I want to do more than just say love words. I want to show you how much I love you, not just tell you!

Luke

Joyita,

   I will dream about you every day and night (which I already do) in nature and the peace and quiet that time has afforded me to think about you. The fluttering of the leaves remind me of angels' wings in the fall breeze and you! As you are a vision of a beautiful angel! The sun shining on my face which reminds me of warmth! I hope you are aware of all that you mean to me and how much I miss you every day! I know it's hard for you to have this time alone with no contact, as it is for me, but I would not abandon or leave you! You are a part of my life and I will send you texts or letters whenever I get service!

                                        Luke

Joyita,

I have been wondering if such happiness is not a dream. It seems to me what I feel is not earthly. I still can't understand this suddenly, cloudless sky. All my soul is yours. Why is there no other word for this, other than joy? Is it because human speech does not have the power to express so much happiness? I fear that I will suddenly wake up from this divine dream. Oh! Now, you are mine! You are finally mine! Soon in a few months, perhaps, my angel will sleep in my arms. She will wake up in my arms, she will live here in my arms forever.

All your thoughts, all the time, all your looks will be for me; all my thoughts, all the time, all my looks will be for you! I will send and receive each one with a lot of love—as I always do, my love. And I always will as we travel though this wonderful life full of love for each other.

With all my love,
Luke

Joyita,

You are the perfect person in the wrong distance. I wish you were here with me, or I there with you.

It is amazing how far you are and how close I feel to you. There is no greater proof of love as loving at a distance. You put your courage, your fidelity, your trust to the test and, above all, your love for that person who makes me smile and who makes me smile just by writing me. That is how you make me feel, my love.

As I float on this ocean of love I keep for you and only you, I sometimes feel like two ships passing in the night. A ship passing another one and that we have missed our mooring and cannot spend our allotted time together, where we were destined to dock. Now, we have to travel this lonely sea, wondering where our true love may be? Where are they at this very moment in time, and what are they doing at this moment in time? So it is, every moment of my day or night. I am thinking of my true love and what is she doing without me. What fun we could be having together instead? I mean she is like a robot that disappears continually from my sight.

I can't touch her or see her in person, so do I need to replace her batteries or give her a recharge kiss? Or possibly plug into her to recharge? I need to worry about her welfare in such ways because she has to keep up with me! She gives me these little power jolts in the form of love signals that I cannot resist, and her love charms are so many I have to make a list!

So it is like being in outer space in a space capsule, waiting to return to Earth and see the one you have missed for so long! I mean if you are in outer space long enough, a robot can look pretty good! But then you are a very, very good looking robot! Ha Ha!

Luke

Good morning, my love.

I am always happy to write my thoughts. Nothing makes me happier than having you with me, and it is very important to for me to know that we can be together . Thanks to life for having one more day of health, for seeing the sun, and knowing that I can see you, love. Nothing would make me happier than to give you a sweet kiss at this moment. Thank you very much for being the two of us together. You are my soulmate, and I only wish to have the opportunity to be sharing together in love and life! I love you!

Joyita

Luke,

Could I accompany you on one of your trips? I agree that to hunt an animal in a safe and humane way without the animal feeling some kind of pain would be the only way to do it. They live in the wild condition and suffer from disease and starvation, but I am in agreement when hunting, they must be killed quickly without suffering. I know in the past, I have seen seal hunters hitting them in the head on TV with blows, which was very ugly. I know you do not let what animals you hunt suffer, and I would like to come along and learn about hunting and what you do. I will enjoy the bonfires at night, camping in the light of the moon, and gazing at the stars together. Burning or rather toasting marshmallows would be a great plan I will enjoy!

Joyita

Luke,

My love, I really value so much the person you are with me. It is important for me to know that I am a jewel for you, and to have the fortune of being with you.

Thank you for giving me all the love in the world! We will be together and always in love. I will enjoy being by your side and to be with you, helping you with your projects like building your small house or storage shed as you call it, making love, and so forth. Thank you for being my man and being by my side. It is so beautiful to read your words when you are away.

Your words that fill me with love and happiness.

Joyita

Joyita,

I don't know how it's is even remotely possible that no man has discovered what a jewel you are! That is why my love name for you is Joyita (little Jewel) is so appropriate! You surprise me every day with some little things about you I did not know or even guess! The result is in my falling in love with you more every day! I think to myself: how could I love this woman any more than I do because my heart is so full of love for her? But then you totally surprise me that you want to try something I love to do, and I fall more in love with you! You are my princess! You are a truly a gem, and I love you for it!

Luke

Good morning my love,

I am happy to see your beautiful letter and I know that every day you get up wishing to have me close to you. It is important for me to know you are happy, and you are still hoping to get together soon. Every day I always get up with a purpose, and the purpose is having you with me, to be able to travel or at least meet together.

I will run into your arms, kiss you passionately, look into your eyes, and smile as my heart is melted with yours. God is too great to not let us meet when you and I feel this great love together. Soon we will see our dreams come true, I want you to know that you have me, and I do not plan to leave. We will only be together—you and me!

Jonita

Joyita,

As I told you before, my words and feeling come from the heart as I know yours do. And I was thinking about what a friend of mine said, "I can never think of what to say at my wife's birthday or anniversary." Or, he never knows what to say to his wife for their anniversary or birthday even though he loves her with all his heart, and such a book would give him ideas of words to use to express himself to her. So, I thought, it would be good to write a book with copies of love letters so people could extract some words of love out of them and use them in letters or on special occasions.

But the main thing I wanted to tell you is I miss you and love you. I am always thinking of you and love your more than words can say. Love you to infinity and back!

All my love,
Luke

Joyita,

To see the sunrise with you many times, I woke up with no spirit, but today I have the best positive energies. I have many cravings for a sweet kiss; how did you sleep last night? I would enjoy having you close to me. I would like to show you how valuable you are to me and for you to feel the affection of my heart. I will be your refuge, your shoulder to cry on, your arms to sleep on, and your lips to kiss. I feel lucky to find you! What are your hobbies? It is always important to for me to know every detail about you. It is important for us to both be open minded, to know each other, to travel, to explore, to live, to feel loved. I only wish you to have a beautiful day! God bless and hope to see you later!

I cannot find any way to fall asleep because I am thinking about you, my dear. I hope to dream about you tonight. If you feel something on your cheek or on your lips when you are sleeping, do not be scared; it is my kiss good night that demonstrates my love for you. Always remember that you are present in my thoughts all day; do not believe that I am exaggerating. When I'm not with you, I feel content to remind you how I miss you. Have sweet dreams, my beloved. Thank you for making this day unforgettable. Thanks for your great idea of writing a book on love and helping other people. I really like very much that we seek this way and help others in love.

Luke

Luke,

    I know how much I like to write you letters, and that is why today I encourage myself to capture my feelings once again on these lines that I know would have been so unhappy if I could not have earned your love, but now I am the happiest woman in the world with you!

    Because you and I are together and because we can be together building a better future, maybe we can even build the treehouse I always dreamed of! I know you will make modifications in your life so we can be together as I will in mine. Only you manage to make me write letters, and let me talk about what I feel, what I dream, what I want in life, only you know who I actually am. I love you for giving me the chance to know you, and everything you do makes me really happy!

Joyita

Joyita,

Whoa, thank you very much for such a beautiful text. Lol—you made me laugh at the last. I love a man who is funny and romantic at the same time! I know the feeling is mutual because I really think of you in the morning, in the afternoon, and at night. I would be talking with you all the time, know your fears, your thoughts, your desires—and correspond in all possible ways to achieve great things with you. You are a wonderful man whom I will never regret meeting.

I had a dream last night that I sat at a huge campfire, eating the world's largest marshmallow, and when I woke up in the morning my pillow was gone! Yuck!

Luke

Hello Luke,

You already know my name, Joyita. I write this letter to you, unique and especially for you! I want to know if you already have a girlfriend? I want to be the owner of your thoughts and be your highest priority. I want to go back to fall in love with you. I want to know if you are also looking for a stable relationship. I am looking for a serious and mature man like you. I long for you and to have a home with you, having a family like I was raised. You will be my family. Every night I will give myself body and soul to you. I am quite passionate. Do you believe that I can have an opportunity with you? We can dialogue about it but please answer this love letter.

Kisses,
Joyita

Hello my love,

I want to make it clear to you from the first moment: I still love you and will not stop doing it. There are no such bad moments that they are going to bring us down. May you never forget that we can do everything together. We have to gather strength and go for it all. You know that when we lean on each other, there is no gale that can beat us. Holding hands, we are stronger than any wall. For this reason, we cannot let that strength escape, thanks to which we will be able to get together and beat all storms that come before us. Love songs for Joyita:

I want to love you, simply—as a word that was never uttered by the wood to the fire that made it ashes. I want to love you simply as a sign that no clouds could send the rain that makes you disappear. When love calls me, I will follow her even if the road is winding and if the sword hidden under her wings pierces the heart of my heart. The body has desires that we do not know; we are separated for worldly reasons to the Ends of the Earth. However, my soul continues to love you until death drags me face to face with the Creator.

Love you,
Luke

Luke,

When I wake up in the middle of the night, I try to get closer to you slowly to feel you. In this way, it gives me the feeling that any moment you are going to appear in my dreams. Where will we travel tonight? Could it be a desert island? Or, maybe we will appear in the mountains? Will it be a night of nightmares? As I write this little text, I see you resting in our bed. It is taking me a lot to fight against that magnet that attracts me with all the force of the universe. I already count the hours to go back to sleep next to you. Good morning, my love. Today, I know that it will be the best day because I will have you by my side. I love you. Have a happy day!

Joyita

Luke,

    Maybe my day is bad, that you find a small failure or the greatest of successes. Problems, obstacles, and disappointments will appear. But thanks to you, I have enough energy to face all difficulties. Life is blessing us with a new day together. It is wonderful that God loves us so much to give us this gift. Open your eyes; I want to sink in them right now. There is no pleasure as to wake up and find you appearing before my eyes or in my mind, and I remember that you are in my life. The first thing I do every morning before opening my eyes is to see if you are here or in my mind. That helps me get up with energy because you are my reason to live. A beautiful day awaits us to enjoy it together. I hope you have a very good day and that you start thinking about me as I am you.

    I am always thinking about you and those two beautiful eyes of yours that are like dark wells I could fall into! I think every day, what did I do right to deserve such a sweet, beautiful woman as you. God must be rewarding me for something I did right! Now that I have heard your sweet voice, I hear it over and over again in my head like a sweet song on the wind. I see these beautiful views when I climb mountains and other places that God has made for us to enjoy, but they don't compare to the beautiful person within you! So I say in the morning and the beginning of each day and the end of them, you will always get a kiss from me along with these words and a hug. I love you! So when you start your morning each day, you can think about that! I hope you will be coming here soon so that it will become a reality to enjoy for the rest of our lives.

Kisses and hugs,
Joyita

Luke,

You have become the most important person in my life. You are one of those irremediably, satisfactory priorities that cannot be ignored. I was not going to tell you that before you arrived, I was empty, not that you fill a gap that was missing in me. But, it is true that it is hard for me imagine a life in which you do not participate. You make me happy every day, and your smile is the most powerful source of energy that I have managed to gather. That is why I do not want to change you for anything. I have to thank you for your patience with me because I am aware that sometimes I can be a very complicated person. With your serenity and your hand, you can bring me back to a calm path and the firm steps of life. Your support has been and is vital so we can move forward as a couple.

I have to admit that every time the mobile vibrates, I look for it quickly to check if it is a message of yours. A smile cannot help but escape when I see your name between the notifications. Sometimes, even, I get a little knot in my throat. Like a fool, I wait for me a little so you do not think I've been pining for you. We have to catch strength and go for it all. You know that when we support ourselves, the one in the other, there is no gale that can topple us.

We are firmer than any wall. You are my reason to dream, and I want you to be part of my decisions and desires.

Let's let this love grow without limits or ceilings because we conceive it from the beginning. That is why sometimes I forget to tell you: Never forget; I love you!

Joyita

Jozita,

My best friend, confidant, and lover, I am sorry I could not text because of no internet signal. You think you are complicated because there is no one else like you, and you are a special person and an individual! You are correct when we are together, we can face and solve any problems or storms that come along.

We will focus on a happy and prosperous future together, built on a foundation of love and passion; it will be a very happy one. It only waits your arrival. It is now summer here, but when fall comes, it will get cooler at night and then winter with its cold temperature and snow. I think I told you, but in the month of November, I hunt white-tailed deer. Many years I worked two and three jobs to put my children through college and couldn't do one of my favorite sports (hunting). Of course, if you are here, that may change, or you may come with me. Do not be sad as you're always in my mind and heart!

Luke

Joyita,

You do not know how much I would like to find the exact words that describe everything I feel about you, but I think I would spend my whole life looking for them, and I would never get to express myself how much I love you. But for that, I prefer to let my actions speak for me and that with every day that happens, you would realize that you occupy a really special place inside my heart. All the love that I have inside belongs to you. I fear nothing when I am with you because your love fills me with courage and strength to face life.

Luke

Luke,

Because I have always wanted to be with you, I feel safe, protected, and capable of overcoming any difficulties. I realize the dreams I have had are getting closer and closer because before I met you, everything was different.

Now, I can say it much better because I have experienced what I had never imagined before. My greatest desire is to keep the feeling alive for all eternity, and that has filled me with so much joy and happiness. If you give me the opportunity to be by your side, I guarantee you that you will have me rendered before you as a woman in love whose only desire will be to see you smile and make you happy. Although life costs us all, just give me the opportunity to love you to give you everything you desire that you once only dreamed of and make you feel what you always wanted.

I would like to get married in the future on an altar before God as my judge of my love for you. Only He knows how I wish to be by your side forever!

Joyita

Luke

I want to be with you, sharing unique moments with your family and that you teach me things that I have not lived or experienced! I want you to embrace me so hard that we only exist you and me, that this love and this flame that we have in our interior lasts always and is never ending.

Because my greatest fear is losing you and being away from you. I would not do anything to get away from you because you are my reason for joy and happiness! I just want to be by your side and that you always love me very strongly.

Joyita

Joyita,

I do love you very strongly and want nothing more than to have you by my side. You are like the air I breathe in that I cannot survive without you! I hug my pillow very closely and my pillow knows your name because I hug it and say it ever night and morning! I think I have told you this before, but I wanted to make sure. I know you were looking for an answer about marriage. We have been together for seven months, and I think in another six months we should plan for it as you have given me your answer, and now that we are engaged, it seems appropriate. Also we are the best team being together so we should make it permanent! I hope you have a fun, relaxing weekend. I love you!

Kisses and hugs!
Luke

Joyita,

What a joy for me, for having met an angel like you on the way, who brightens my days and makes me appreciate every second that life gives me. I thank destiny for having placed you before me, because with you, I have the opportunity to be truly happy. All my love is for you because from the moment I saw you, I knew that I would not find a face so perfect that it would be a softer, sweeter smile than yours. You are everything I have always dreamed of and that beautiful dream became a wonderful reality the day I met you. Since then, I have not stopped thinking about you and the immense desire I have to be by your side. Knowing that I still have a lot to discover, I confess I fell in love with you. My days are happier if you are in them, and everything that surrounds you acquires a more beautiful meaning when I see you pass in front of me. That is to say, that you are like a ray of sunlight that illuminates everything and everyone around you without even making an effort. And if I am honest with myself, this is what I love most about you.

Luke

Good morning love,

To be able to have you close to me, I love that you dream of me and we can enjoy a lot of all the love possible. Thank you for giving me your true love. Every day I am happier than the previous one because of you. It is important to me that we can afford to transmit a great love. I am full of happiness with you, I really enjoy having you close to me. We will be together, and I just hope that we can give each other a sweet kiss that lasts an eternity!

Luke

Luke,

It is surprising that together we can do things well and that we now have a plan to be able to create a business of a website to help people in love. We can also share more of our love letters and history and serve as an example for people who wish to be together. It is a wonderful idea to make a book out of our love letters. I feel very excited to share more of my words and affection for you. You are the best thing that has happened to me in my life and the source of my inspiration.

Joyita

Joyita,

I have a wish to hide in that wonderful smile of yours. Let me discover that new world that smiles in your eyes, a new world made with all the colors of the rainbow, a new world that, from the first steps, shows me who I can trust to savor life. All I ask of you is a dream that transports us from sky to sea, like the sun rises every dawn, a dream of infinite love, a dream that takes us far.

Hide my love in your arms, put your mouth on mine, and we will travel through all the love in the world. Just for me tonight, let me rest in your huge eyes because I can't love you more than that, letting your warmth and arms caress me, for I am as close to heaven as I can get here on earth!

Luke

Joyita,

You are too sweet with your words and your beauty, not only on the outside, but your inner beauty supersedes it and makes you the treasure you are! How could I find you in this place with so many distractions in life, except you shine like a star! It is like I was looking for a plant but found the most beautiful flower in the garden of love! You are so much of a treasure that most men search their whole life for and never find. But here you are, right in front of me. The best part is to recognize what a find you are and not let you get away!

Luke

Luke,

Your eyes are my stars, and your arms are my bandages, and your kisses my cure. Because I have had a great time, but now everything is happiness that fills me inside that make me think of you at all times and gives me everything I need.

I can blow against the wind and not lose a measure of equilibrium because you hold me and your voice guides me. It gives me hope; it makes me feel the happiest woman in the world.

Joyita

Joyita,

Wow! I saw the picture you sent me—so beautiful! You fill me with love in so many ways, with your beauty and words that have such feeling! You are more than I could ever hope for in a soulmate! You take my breath away! I miss you and love you completely! I am so happy to be in the relationship with you. I have never met a woman like you. You are willing to learn about my hobbies and do so much for me. You really complete me!

Kisses,
Luke

Luke,

   I'm sorry that things at your work are sour, but sometimes things can go like that. I want you to know that I am with you, and I never want to separate from your side. You are someone very important to me, and I want you to teach me, I have learned a lot from you, and every day I feel like the luckiest woman to share such nice moments with you. I would like to be by your side and be able to hug you every day, every night, and every moment. I will never to allow you to leave my side, just as you are doing at the moment. Ha Ha Ha!

   I want to be by your side every day of my life. I want to see you because your looks and personality fill me with joy and make my days happier. You always fill me with love. You are my special love, and I want to spend my whole life in your arms, stealing your kisses. I cannot wait until we are back together again.

Joyita

Luke,

Hello, my beautiful love!

With every day that passes, I feel very fortunate to have you in my life and that you are my future companion for eternal life. I know that our story had not started much, but I am sure that we will write the best love story that ever existed in the world.

You are the person who has the incredible gift of making me smile at any moment. You always brighten my day with just one smile or message. You are so special; you became the man who managed to captivate my heart.

Joyita

Joyita,

You are my dream woman, not only beautiful on the outside, but more beautiful on the inside. You are always sweet, and I am sure you have that furious, hating temper, but I love all of you! You are correct; we will live the best love story ever! I love you and miss you with all my heart! I can't wait until you arrive so I can hug you and kiss you again in person.

Luke

Luke,

I never imagined that you were going to fall in love with me, and you would begin to take the first step to achieve my love when you had already done it. It has been a long time since you and I met, and I can assure you that my feelings for you are so special; every moment that I have spent by your side is something unforgettable. You make me feel like a true queen in your castle.

I love you for being so special with me and for loving me like that. I promise you that I will fight for our love and have a future together as a couple. I will always love you as long as God allows it, my love. I love you.

Joyita

Luke,

I am not asking that you respond to this. I am telling you today with a love letter because I know that it is not easy to say what you feel in person. But if one day you see me and want to answer me, do it with a kiss or a caress, and I will understand that, like me, you to have fallen hopelessly in love. My heart beats stronger every time I see you. Every time I listen to you, every time I think of you, and they have told me this is how it happens when someone important enters your life to smite you with their love.

I confess that I have fallen in love with you and that although I had never expected it because of the fear of being hurt or betrayed, I do not regret having fallen into the game of love. You, my darling, are the one who has won my heart. What has happened to me is truly magical, and although sometimes I feel that I am losing my mind, I do not care as long as it is for you and for the immense love that you make me feel.

Joyita

Luke,

I never thought I would say it, but Cupid has struck my heart! I know this because when I see you, my heartbeat accelerates. My hands sweat, and I start to studder. That is something that only happens to those who are in love. Therefore, today I confess that you are the owner of my heart, and I give you everything I feel and what I am in this love letter! I want to tell you that in my heart, there is a special place that I reserve for you. I have not come to feel what you have caused in me because of anyone, and that I know that it is a good love. I am writing you this love letter because I want to express everything that I have inside and hope it is worth the attempt to make you confess if you feel the same for me as I feel for you.

Because nothing would make me happier than knowing that you have fallen in love with me.

Joyita

Joyita,

It was a day like any other but I will never forget the date. We coincided without thinking about time or space. Something magical happened. I was caught by your smile. You stole my heart without permission. And, so without telling us anything, in a single look, our love began. You changed my life.

Since you came to me, you are my sun that illuminates my entire existence. You are a perfect dream. I find everything in you. You changed my whole life. It is because of you that I believe in love again. Now only your lips light up my skin. Today there are no doubts here, the fear left me, all thanks to you. You are so beautiful on the outside, like no one on earth. And, inside, you live the nobility and goodness of love. Today the word *love* has another dimension for me. Day and night I ask heaven to watch over both of us. Now everything is so clear: it is you I love. You gave me the illusion. You changed my life for the better.

Since you came to me. You are the sun that illuminated my entire existence. You are a perfect dream. It is because of you I have believed that there are no doubts and the fear left me. All thanks to you!

Luke

Luke,

We are good enough to each other to know what has happened with time and distance. Now that we are together much more, one more additional month for seven total. We are amazing together, much more than apart. In the future, we will get married. We will be happy, and everything will revolve around our family, you and me. We will take care of it and do fantastically, as we are now or even better because we will spend more time together. More than these seven months that become wonderful for us. What a joy to be with you and always accompanied by you! Thank you for everything you give me. Thank you for being who you are, and thank you for your love. We will always be together; do not hesitate. I just want you to project your wedding idea to me and make it the best for you and for both of us too. I just want you to be happy by my side and see that you are actually the man with whom I will live my best years. Have your got a honeymoon place in mind? It is important to always be one step ahead of life and we will be great.

Kisses for my dear,
Joyita

Joyita,

You are not only the most beautiful woman on the outside, but the way you communicate your beautiful feelings on the inside makes you even more beautiful, if that can be possible! I have found the sweetest fruit in the garden of love, and it is you! God must be rewarding me for something because I have found the treasure every man searches for his whole life but never finds. That treasure is you! I cannot wait to taste your lips on mine or hug you tightly and tell you how I feel in person!

Love you,
Luke

Joyita,

To see in time the desire to love and be loved, pursuing the star that lights up your life, living in the memory of a lost love, bravely continuing the fight in the infinite darkness envelops the body. A memory emerges in my mind of a fire before going out that slowly, slowly, slowly, ignites again.

I have a wish to hide in that wonderful smile of yours.

Luke

Joyita,

There is no established occasion to tell someone you care about their well-being because any time is the best time. People should have the possibility of getting the best phrases and texts, or letters of love, on a page that we believe we can give them. Give them the right words to demonstrate their love. When you stay without inspiration, it is difficult between them to find affection in their words. So the book of letters is a great idea to help them. I, myself, look for a photo of you on my computer, and it helps me to write with more sincere feelings for you. I think these ideas will help others indeed.

Luke

Honey,

A book of love letters is a magnificent idea. I feel that we both have a lot of talent and ideas about our love for each other. Our love letters express our deep feelings for each other, and I think our letters have wonderful words and meaning. We always try to use the perfect words to describe how much we love we have for each other. Many people need to see examples for their inspiration, the right words to transform their text or letter into a real masterpiece. When in a love relationship, it is convenient to have good examples and have different means to express love and affection. I hope that we can help couples who want to express their feelings to one another in a simple text or spoken word. My beloved Luke, it is a great idea! Love is a wonderful feeling that should be expressed clearly and nakedly from the heart, at least in writing and words.

Joyita

Joyita,

As I have told you, I want to write a book about our love letters. It will tell about our romance and how we express love to each other. This is so people can get ideas or be inspired for a text by using our examples and what they feel in their hearts! Many people, especially men, want to express their feeling to a loved one but do not know how. This gives them an example or helps them choose the right words. It may help them to say the words they have been searching for on a special occasion.

So I want to ask you: what you think? Communication is very important, and you are a part of me and this idea, so your opinion matters very much. How would you feel about doing this? I feel the love letters or texts we write are beautiful and have a lot of feeling that we could share with others. I think these letters form the basics of a book about the language of love.

It not only tells our love story and could just be enjoyable reading, but it shows other people how they could express their feelings. Some people just cannot write love letters on their own, so these give great examples of messages from the heart. I just want to check with you because it would mean sharing our feelings with the outside world. I love and miss you so much.

Love always,
Luke

Joyita,

Every day I get to know you more and more, and I believe that we will be perfect and happy together—almost certainly. I also think that excessive displays of affection overwhelm you, so the best thing is that today we do not do much more, just spend a wonderful day together. As we do every day, we see each other, we love each other, and we kiss each other. Love is the meaning of us both, that I assure you is real. And today I don't want to do anything too big. I want to give you this love letter that comes from my heart so that it can reach your head and your heart. If I look you in the eyes and try to tell you, I will forget everything I want to say. Of course, in our life, many things have happened, some have been a little harder and others have been much softer, but these two months have been much softer. They have been like a calm to my old day-to-day routine of what happened to me before you.

Before you, everything was much worse; everything was different. Now I am happy and I can say it in an incredible way that I never thought would happen to me. Thanks to you, I have found happiness, and I think that is how people's lives should always be, but unfortunately, it is not always like that. They have hurt us so much in the past. We both know that. But it has already happened and we have overcome it to be together. Therefore, let's not celebrate these two months; let's celebrate the years. I just hope that we can always enjoy things and that we never lack health. Thousands of hugs for you, and I hope this is the best day of your life with many more to come!

Tell me more, I want to know every detail about you as it makes for a stable relationship when you know more good things about the other person. I love you.

Luke

Luke

My dearest man! I'm ready to follow you to the ends of the earth. I would have wiped off two thousand pair of shoes and continued on my way barefoot, bumping into rocks and rubbing my feet in blood for you. I would never have complained to you because I would have been very happy. Because with you, because next to you, hand in hand for the rest of our days and beyond, I would help you not to stumble.

I would support you in moments of sadness.

I would never give you a reason to doubt yourself.

I would not say many words about love; I would just love you with all my heart, with all my soul, as no woman has every loved any man on this earth. I wanted to give you my heart forever. I would have followed you with my eyes closed, forgetting my previous life before you, zeroing it out completely.

I was ready to follow you to the ends of the earth. If you would only call me to follow.

Will you call me to the end of the world? Will you touch me to you?

Do you love me like I love you? Waiting for your answer!

Joyita

Joyita,

I dreamed I was hugging you all night long, but when I woke up I was hugging my pillow! HA! HA! Now you may think you can be replaced by a pillow! But, no! Although the pillow is quieter, I miss your lips to kiss!

Luke

Luke,

I hope to continue living experiences with you. I wish that your hand and mine would never leave each other. I long for your look to be the light that motivates me to always follow. I want you to be someone who is always with me. I love to receive all of your love, my dear beloved Luke. I really want to be by your side. I hope you listen to this song by Foreigner, "I Want to Know What Love Is." I want you to show me what your love is.

Love you always,
Jozita

Luke,

I am pleased to love you. I enjoy caressing you and going to sleep with you. It is thrilling to have you face to face and make you smile. I would give anything for always being here with you. To let me love you, give yourself to me, and I will not fail you. I want to grow old with you, kiss you, and lose my time with you. I will keep your secrets, take care of your moments, hug you, wait for you, adore you, and have patience with you. Your madness is my science; I enjoy to look at every movement that I have a pleasure, a value you never forget. You give me back many times, and I will not fail you.

I adore you,
Joyita

Joyita,

Maybe I still do not know all the difficulties that come with a lifetime commitment, but I have enough in relationships to know what I want and how I imagine my life with the person with whom I will commit myself.

You know we will have to organize the expenses of a wedding very well, but we can keep things in order because the love we have always is much stronger than anything before us.

Those friends and relatives that surround me are a continuous source of inspiration and how I want our relationship to be. So here, today, I promise to try to give my best efforts always.

Luke

Joyita,

My love, that is all anyone can ask is to make your best effort. As I have told you before, so will I make my best effort. Thank you for your commitment and love. I must tell you, you make me so very happy, and I am so honored by your love and affection for me. You will also receive my best effort and commitment to always respect you, be faithful, and love you with all of my being.

I also have to tell you I tried watching *One Hundred Human Feet* on Netflix, but it was not available here. Also, I was listening to old love songs, and these reminded me of you, "Baby Love" by the Supremes, "Stuck on You" by Lionel Richie, "At Last" by Etta James, and "Be My Baby" by the Rondells. I hope you are having a good day and everything is going your way.

Love and miss you,
Luke

Joyita,

My love, I wanted talk about our wedding and honeymoon as you have mentioned it in your letter, but I want to talk to you in person about it. After talking in detail, we will decide together how it will be and where. You may want to do it at your home city so your family can attend. We need to talk over such things. Then we will decide where we will go on a honeymoon. Of course, costs will be discussed and a budget to set everything up. We don't want to start out with a lot of debt. I am sure we can plan and save to do it very well. You are my treasure and worth every penny we spend.

I also want to tell you I have missed you these days so I am writing to let you know. Your texts and letters are so expressive and filled with such love and passion that I fall in love with you more each day. I am so lucky to have you in my life, and I love you very, very much!

Luke

Luke,

I have awakened serene, with good energy to start writing to you today. If it is necessary to write a daily text or letter, I would do it so that you would realize the love that I feel for you. I know you must be impressed to know that a woman who is truly delivering everything for you will write to you. But I also know you have not thought about why I do it. Well, you are a very incredible man, and that is the truth. I am very surprised by the ability you have to communicate, and more than anything I want you to know that you are the man I am looking for. You make me the happiest woman in the world. I really hope that we can always get along in the best way. I wish I could understand you in the best way. Everything in life is achieved with effort, and I know that winning your heart was an achievement. I never want you to stop your feelings for me. I just know that I can always count on you and that you will never reject me. As time goes by, you will continue to choose me each time. I just hope we both always spend our lives this way. I hope you have a good time by my side and long life with me.

Many kisses,
Joyita

Luke, my love,

I hope to apologize about yesterday. It was a very busy day for me; I really feel it was the most busy day of my life. Yesterday, I closed some business with some project agents with whom I have been working lately. Then at night, I had to attend a dinner meeting. They made a special reservation for me to discuss the final details and to close the deal.

I have missed you a lot. Maybe I am telling you too much, but I missed you this morning because you are so cute with me. You always paint a smile on my face and illuminate me with the light you place in my heart. You don't know how much I would like to be with you now and be able to tell you how much I love you. I appreciate you, and I have you presently in my heart. You have me so in love that you are the last thing I think about before sleeping, and the first thing I think about in the morning.

Joyita

Joyita,

Good morning my beautiful love. I couldn't wait to talk to you as I have missed your loving words as I miss the sun when it sinks out of sight to become the night. Night is when I miss you most, as I am laying in my bed thinking about you and how I want to hold you in my arms and shower you with kisses. But I know that day is coming soon, as you say our time together is coming, and this time of loneliness is passing quickly. But your arrival can never be quick enough for me. I just wanted to send this short text to let you know how much I love you. Also, I want to let you now I really appreciate all the love you have for me. I wanted to say that you honor me with that love and affection, and I will love you until the bitter end.

Love,
Your Luke

Luke,

It seems hard to believe, but we have been together for a long time, which has helped us to know much more about each other and to be able to share wonderful moments of your life. I remember what my life was like before I met you (but only vaguely now!), not that I ever want to return to those sad times and that existence. It was at that time I did not expect much of love. But then you came like a light to enlighten me, since you came into my life, changing it completely for the better.

Time has passed very fast, and we have planned our encounter to be together, to build a future, and buy things for our little home so that we do not lack anything when we are together. I thank God we are united to each other.

Joyita

Luke,

It is a sunny day, and I feel good energy on this beautiful day. I hope that we can always speak with confidence in the world. I know that we have spoken a few times, but it is important to always get to know each other, to learn more, and above all give each other an account of all that we can find to express our feelings to know how good they are and be in constant chemistry. I am happy to know that you arrived on an important day of my life. We can never fill life with pain; on the contrary, we must always deliver joy and positive energy as well. I know that you understand very well and can realize everything in life you can do to be happy. Do you want to know me better in person in the future? I hope you do. I hope you agree to make decisions together, think things through, and you will see that everything can go your way.

A big hug for you!
Joyita

Luke,

You are the person who is and will always be by my side, despite everything that could happen. You are the person with whom I want to share the good and the bad moments of my life and the person with whom I will share beautiful memories. You are the person that I love at this moment and forever. I want to tell you what I feel, and I want to thank you for all you have done to make my life much better. You tell me the kind of things that a woman needs and wants to hear. You also think about things that I need or want to make my everyday life better, like new pillows, sheets, towels, and places to put all my shoes and clothes. It turns our small apartment into our home. But the most important thing is we are together and share the little details that life gives us.

Joyita

Joyita,

Yes, of course I think of your comfort and well-being, as that is a part of love and a relationship. Thinking about the other person is paramount and a sign of affection. So now you learn more about me and how I really feel about you. I hope it make you more at ease about coming here.

The only other thing we need other than pillows and sheets are towels, shampoo, soap—the things that you use or prefer and will pick out the colors you prefer. I want us to shop together to not only enjoy the time together, but the thought of using the items brings back memories of the experience and the time spent together. I have also built a small counter with a wine rack underneath, as I know you occasionally like wine with dinner.

Love you always,
Luke

My lovely Joyita,

Every day I miss you so much. To have you by my side and drown you in kisses when we go to sleep or wake up is all I can think about because I love you so much. You send me the sweetest love texts and letters I have ever received in my life, which makes me love you even more! That is because I believe what you tell me and say is sincere and truthful. I didn't tell you why I built a storage shed. It is so I can move some things out of my apartment to make room for your clothes, shoes, and so on. I know you will need space for such things. I want you to feel welcome and comfortable. I try to think what I need to do to prepare for your arrival. I already bought some champagne for us to celebrate and some wine to have with dinner on occasion for special nights (although every night you are here is special). I also bought pink pillowcases and sheets and softer pillows as mine are very firm. I do these things always with love. We will go shopping for towels and whatever else we need.

Love you!
Luke

Luke,

I miss you like nothing in this world because you are everything in this world for me. It does not matter how far we are; I always feel like I am by your side. Your lovely looks are still alive in my eyes because I miss you more than anything and because I miss you and love you. I would die tonight for a letter or text on your part. You send me a letter or text, and I then could wait for you for a thousand years, if necessary. Only if you send me a letter or text at this time will I be able to sleep tonight and dream of you.

Joyita

Joyita,

In a world where love is not easy to find, I have been the most fortunate because I have had the immense luck to have encountered you and staying by your side, completely in love. What I now have, I am tightening my grip on so as not to lose it to keep an angel like you who illuminates my days and makes me value every second that gives me life.

I love you my dear,
Luke

Luke,

I've really read your reasons, and I'm seriously impressed with how much you like me, in the most natural way.

My hundreds reasons why I am in love are based on your affection, your respect, and admiration for me. I really just want to have you close to me, and I am more in love with you every day now that I know that you are everything in my life! Every time I see your letter and the reasons why you love me, I fall in love. I will keep that beautiful letter, and I will only wait for the moment that we are together so that you can read it for me. I really thank the universe or God, for our union, our ways together, I align with you, our hearts are in the same direction. You are unconditional, and I am the right woman for you. I really give thanks to life for you. Everything I hope for is to have the certainty of filling you with love. We will be together in love—I hope you give us this opportunity to be happy. Thank you again for writing that letter so full of love because I really know that you write them out of your heart, and nothing can be more sincere than that.

Joyita

Luke,

Only God knows how much I love you and the many sunrises that I live, thinking of you. I just miss imagining your look, your lips, and the curious dimple that is made in your cheek every time you smile. I sigh like a woman in love when I think of the owner of my heart. You are my inspiration, everything that I live for, and every breath I take. Every thought and every feeling has your name engraved on it. Because you have penetrated every space in my soul, and I have come to love you as I have never loved before. As God only knows that I do.

Joyita

Luke,

Good morning love. How sweet it is to see a letter from you. Thank you first of all for always taking the time to write to me. Yesterday I was with my family; I had a great day with them. How was your weekend? Now I'm working, love. Thank God, I don't have much work. Did you sleep last night? We will be together in love; I wish to come to be by your side this moment. I really value the man that you are with me and the patience that you and I have had for me. It is important that you continue to be in love with me, and I am in love with you. I really feel happy to give you the best in the world.

Joyita

Joyita,

I think about you almost two hours a day when we aren't together. I think of that little person who has a heart so big that it appears a few times in a life, or it is simply fate that has united us. I have this knocking on the door of my heart, insisting I open up more and more because it is the only thing I want to do in life. I want to be with you, fly with you, kiss and hug you. Because if time shows it is correct or that time heals, that is what is happening right now—that your eyes are my stars, that your arms are my bandages and your kisses my cure. Because I have had a bad time, but now everything is happiness—the type that fills you inside, the type that makes me think of you at all times and gives me everything I need. I can blow against the wind and not lose an iota of balance because you hold me, and your voice guides me. You give me hope; you make me feel warm even when it is below zero.

Luke

Luke,

I really just want to have the opportunity to be together. Thank you for this beautiful opportunity to meet you. How did you feel when first meeting me? I just want you to give me the opportunity to be together. I want to give life the opportunity to get along, that there is that trust that we look for in a person. Actions are often better than words.

I have the expectation that we can take the next step—you know what I mean? I want this love to be consolidated, all I hope is to give us the opportunity to be happy.

Thanks for always being with me! I hope you are the right man that whenever you gets up next to me, you looks at me with love and without losing the shine from your eyes.

What I want the most is to fill you with love, just waiting for us to be together! I hope this letter makes you smile and fills your heart with happiness.

Joyita

Luke,

Awakening without your kisses fills me with anguish because there are no better dawns than those when we awake together, and I can know that there is someone in my life, who always expects that we do as much as possible to show our love with these letters as in antiquity that vanished before the look of others. It is so romantic for you, my Luke, the one you always have words of love and breath in the sad days for me.

Today, I have woken up without you. I am writing to tell you that you are the person that I adore and appreciate in all the world, my beloved Luke.

Joyita

Luke,

Thank you for being the owner of my heart. You are a person who always lives with that beautiful smile on your face, always transmitting joy, a person who fights for what he wants. You are that person who makes me fall in love more and more every day and who is capable of melting anyone with his eyes. You are the person who will always be by my side, despite everything that may happen, and the person with whom I share and will share beautiful memories. Person I love right now, I want to tell you how I feel, and I want to thank you for everything. It's good to know that you can achieve many things, I just want you to feel that I am grateful to spend time next to a man who makes the world stop for a second. How do you enjoy kissing?

My favorite hobbies riding a motorcycle, tennis, gym. What are yours?

Joyita

Joyita,

    You sent me a picture with that smile of yours that melts my heart! I can tell you it makes me miss you that much more because I just want to hold you in my arms, hug you, and never let you go! I love you more than life itself, so you never have to worry about other women. You are my woman, my love, and the one who completes me! Only you have the magic power to suck up my soul and keep it in your heart! As for my heart, it is already yours and has your name engraved in it. So, you see, you have me completely. I cannot live without you! Without you I only exist!

    I send you love signals all day long from my mind to yours! I hope you can feel them! I know how you like a love letter, and I love to send them. I know what you mean about consummating our love, and I promise we will be engaged when you come, if you grant me permission to marry you after meeting me in person. Then we will get married in six months in your home city so your family can attend. I also hope to go there soon so your family can meet me.

Luke

My beautiful, sexy, sweet Joyita,

I would not find another flower like you in the garden of love if I searched my whole life. You bring such joy to my heart and soul that I cannot even express it all. I am so fortunate to have found you or that you found me. I am so in love with you, it is almost like I have never loved before because each day you write me, you make me fall more in love with you. I did not think it was possible to love someone as much as I love you. But each day, I love you even more than the day before. I think when you get here, you will be in grave danger of being eaten by my kisses! I know it has been seven months, and I don't know how much longer, but you are worth the wait. So I must miss you a little more each day until your arrival. But anything you want to know about me, just ask—and if you ask, I will answer.

Love you,
Luke

Luke,

I always wished to have a good man, honest, humble and loving, by my side, who would accompany me in each of my days and give me his unconditional love, support, both in my sorrows and in my joys. Today I'm lucky enough to say that I have found that man and that I am fortunate to have him by my side, giving me all the love that I have always dreamed of—and that is my most beautiful reality. That man is you, darling, and I want to thank for having crossed my path on my way and have given me all tenderness and your loyalty. I hope that destiny always keeps us united and that we are together for all eternity because I want us to marry. I hope that we have the best marriage in history, as we have planned to make two weddings, which would be best to be with your family and with mine because I want this to be as special for you as for me. My heart feels all the world's love for you is something I admire because I never think about feeling all this love that now is for you.

Joyita

Joyita,

    I am so much in love that you are the last thing I think about before going to bed and the first thing I think about every morning. I wish you a good day every morning because I never want you to forget that I think about you, and I want you to have a good time until the end of the day. I also want to give you my sincere love, hug you, and comfort you because you are my beloved. I hope you have had sweet dreams from the night before and your rest has been comforting—and that this morning you have risen with the best mood.

    I woke up thinking about you, loving you, and missing you ever so much. You are the most important person that has ever happened to come into my life. I hope this letter of good wishes lets you know how much I love you.

Luke

Luke,

Your letters are always warm and full of compassion. In the journey of life, it is good to meet people who really care about you. You are the man who I want to spend the rest of my life because you love me for what I am and not for what I have in life. It is too beautiful, and I thank you for allowing me to enter your life every day. You make me the happiest woman in the world and have caused me many pleasant sensations to be by your side. I hope you never doubt my love and the good intentions I have for you. Because I could never see you far away from me for a minute more, and my heart cannot take the distance that separates us. This distance is not an obstacle because every "I love you" reminds me that we are one for the other, my love.

Your constant actions for our love surprise me and fill me with warmth in my heart. You have always made me your company and have let me lean on you when things were difficult. You always do everything so that we are happy.

Joyita

My beloved Luke,

A couple of days ago, I saw a film which said that protagonist had a theory about moments of impact. My theory about these moments of impact is these moments of intense flashes that change life forever. They end up defining us. And I feel that you were like that miracle that came into my life to stay and define myself. I am so in love with you that it is crazy because before, I did not want to be with anyone, but you entered my life and I found you a miracle of life. I know I'll stay with you for the rest of my life. You always are aware of my tastes and what I recommend, so you really listen to me. I like that you investigate and research and make an effort to see what I like. The movie I recently watched is *One Hundred Human Feet*, which is very grotesque and a little bloody but a very good movie. You are my treasure that I love most in my life.

Joyita

Joyita,

It is interesting how movies and books can sometimes affect how we think and feel about our lives and relationships. That is the desired effect the author or director is trying to get across to their audience. So I am in total agreement with your opinion. I am also afraid with all these texts or letters you are making me fall hopelessly in love with you!

I will see if I can find the series, *Money Heist,* and watch it so we can discuss it. I like that you are not only beautiful but also have a good head on your shoulders to hold an intelligent conversation. I always love your texts or letters because they are heartwarming and intelligent with such good expression and use of language with feeling.

You make me feel very comfortable talking with you. I love and cherish that about you. It shows your maturity and honest feeling in which we match very well.

I love you always,
Luke

Luke,

You are one of the most important and indispensable people in my life. You have taught me what love is. It is hard for me to imagine a life without you because you are everything I want and desire. You make me the happiest woman, just by telling me those beautiful words and show me that by your side, I can be the luckiest woman to have you. I appreciate your patience, your serenity, and your helping hand because you manage to guide me on my gray days. Your support has been very important for me to move on. You have been my best decision and my great reason to dream. Let this love continue to grow without limits because only you and I know that our love is much greater than anything. The book you wrote is the most wonderful representation of our love life. I love you immensely, and I loved your beautiful list of things you love about me.

Joyita

Luke,

Close your eyes my love, I want you to feel that soft and delicate kiss that I am sending you. There is a big "miss you" on the way. Love in this life you will never know, nor will you ever imagine how far I will go, nor what I would be able to do to have your love.

My love, do not be afraid to let me enter your little heart, do not be afraid or doubt my love for you. Do not think that one day I will leave you and leave our life. I will always be there for you, in me you can trust, in me you will always find our faithful company, our confidant, in me you will always be, but above all, in me you will always find the love of your life!

Joyita

Hello, my love,

This day is as special as you. Do you know why? Because the sun shines with as much intensity as your eyes do when you are happy and because the air smells of your charming aroma. My love, I send you the best vibes from here and wish you the best so that you have a great day, my heaven. Darling, do not let anyone erase your beautiful smile from your face; do not let anyone make you lose your good mood. Do not let anyone steal the happiness for which we have been fighting for so long.

Always show the best of you to the world from the start of day until it ends. My life, let us not forget to thank God for allowing us to have one more day with life and health, and for allowing us to be together to continue loving each other and to be able to continue fighting with all our strength for this great love that unites us by giving us the ray of light every morning to warm and illuminate our hearts. Despite the problems we have, a beautiful smile always prevails over us.

Luke

Luke,

I am so sure of you, so sure that I want you to be the man of my life because by your side I have found everything my life needs. You are the ideal man, the perfect man, the most beautiful creature that God has put in my way. I want you to be the man of my life because in you I encounter affection, sweetness, understanding, and sincerity. I love you so much that I do not even know how to tell you with words how much I adore you, and you will always be the best stage of my life. I will always wait for you, even if it is centuries, years, decades, and so forth. My love, I believe in you and recognize that you will be a great love until the end that no one can ever separate us. I have assembled so many feelings and thoughts about you to keep in my box of secrets and my heart. My love is so great I cannot even think about describing it. Do you think I am crazy to tell you how much you mean to me? Have you ever loved a woman like me before?

Joyita

Luke,

    You are the most special person I know, and I do not say it just because I am your girlfriend. I say it because it is the truth. I have not found another person like you, ever. And I have never felt this way about another person. Every time I think about you, my heart races out of control. I cannot believe when I receive your letter or text from you how it fills me with so much joy. The beautiful words you send make me so happy that you are thinking about me. You are a dream that I never want to wake up from. The best part is that you are with me, accompanying me, and making my sad days turn into something beautiful. Do I really deserve this love that is so pure and real from you?

Joyita

Joyita, Hello, Love,

I am writing to you in this letter what I have wanted to tell you for a long time. I want to tell you but I couldn't do it face to face because I get caught up in your gaze, I am distracted by your lips, and I wrap myself in your smile. And then I forget to tell you. You must know that I am so happy with you because you make me laugh, because you make me tremble, because you make me dream. I notice your respect, your acceptance of my hobbies and my passions and because you don't try to change me.

I am so happy with you because by your side, I finally feel that I am part of the world. Because of your way of minimizing problems, because of the complicity that we have created, and because with your "forever," my life has begun to make sense. But above all, I am so happy to be in your embrace. And you know I'm not the best at expressing my feelings, so I'm going to try to tell you the only way I know how. Without poetic license, without metaphors, and without rhyming verses, like this, crudely and brutally: "I love you." And this is how I have to tell you. You are the woman of my life. And I could write it in capital letters because I am certain that is so.

Luke

Luke,

For a long time I waited for a man like you. For many years I thought that love was very difficult to find, but now that you are here, I feel very lucky. That is because I finally found a person who understands the way I feel, who accepts me for who I am, and who is by my side when everyone turns their back on me. Everything seems so different now that I met you. Thank you for being who you are, for being so sweet, and loving me so much and showing me with kisses that love exists. I will return everything in full. You will have my unconditional love, and I will always be there for you. Thank you for appearing in my life; thank you for being my love.

Joyita

Joyita,

You are the person who is and will always be by my side, despite everything that could happen and the person with whom I want to share the good and bad moments of my life. You are the person with whom I share beautiful memories and the person I want to tell what I feel and thank for all I have with you. I have so many words of thanks because you make my life much better. We can shop for the things we need and buy together, like towels, shampoo, and so on. And it will be a fun experience and memory that we do together. We will make our house our home by doing these things. Because the most important thing is that together we share the little details that life gives us.

I love you always,
Luke

My beloved,

As always, you are thinking about my well-being, and when I feel comfortable, I thank you for your love. You make me happy every day, always bringing a smile, affection, your protection, your details, your love, your work, and your effort for us every day. Your support guides the truth that I could continue listing many things that you have brought such many beautiful thoughts to me. You have taught me to smile constantly, and it is something for which I have stayed so far. Thanks for keeping my heart happy. I hope to have a lot of time by your side. I will do everything possible so that every day you fall in love with me, as a way to thank you for everything you do for me.

Joyita

Joyita,

There are a thousand things I want to tell you every morning, a thousand ideas go through my mind when I see your sweet eyes illuminate my world when dawn comes. A thousand sensations run through my body that rests next to yours. A thousand melodies resonate in me when with your sweet voice you tell me, "I love you."

Your smile is my conviction every morning when I see you; you are the face that pushes me to want to be better every day. At sunrise, as I lay next to your body, I smell the perfume of a thousand cherry blossoms. At dawn, I say, "I love you," good morning, one as a thousand kisses are exchanged. Every morning, you touch my soul with our eternal love. Today is the perfect day because I know that you are by my side because with your smile, you illuminate more than the sun. Your eyes are my condemnation and my perdition.

Luke

Luke,

Although I know that everything is like this, I cannot
help dreaming of you, dreaming that we are together at
this moment and that my nights and yours are no longer in
solitude, that solitude which causes sadness that embraces
my soul, my being, and my heart. Making the dreams
escape, and turning my thoughts that only hurt me but also
become memories of moments in which we are together,
in the distance, listening to your warm voice on the phone
when you call me, seeing your sweet and loving face
through the monitor. It is beautiful to hear you say how much
you love me and how much you miss me! How beautiful it is
to know that our love continues to grow day by day! Good
love, what else can I tell you if I have told you everything,
if you fully know that my feelings revolve around you. I love
you more than anyone in life, and distance does not obscure
this love that I feel because it is so great and so deep
that I need to shout it to the whole world. It is impossible
to silence what the heart feels because you know that it
is in this feeling of happiness that having someone by your
side is revealed.

Joyita

Joyita,

   You are the person who is and will always be by my side despite everything that could happen, the person with whom I want to share the good and bad moments of my life, and the person with whom I share beautiful memories. You are the person I love at this moment. I want to tell you what I feel and want to thank you for all I have, with so many words of thanks to you, because you make my life much better with the simple things we do together and memories that we share—these little details that life gives us and most important the feeling of love that comes with them. I highlight both the creative and ingenious things that you do for me.

Luke

Joyita,

What a gift from heaven it is to wake up next to you. What a divine privilege to wake up next to your fragile and ethereal body. What a dream come true to be with love and always have you with me. Good morning, angel of my heart. Thank you for so much sweetness; thank you for so much love. For you I would give everything— my body and soul. For you I give my life and my karma. I fall in love with you in my early mornings. I give everything to you every morning and night; I surrender myself.

With much love always!

Luke

My love,

Waking up without your kisses filled me with anguish because there are no better sunrises than the ones I wake up next to you, with the smell of your hair, the warmth of your hugs and the calming sound of your words. Your voice in the morning is the best melody. Today that I have awakened without you; I understand how much I miss you. I am writing to wish you a good day and remind you how much I love you, sweetheart. I hope to see you soon so I can wish you good morning with a hug and a kiss.

Luke

Luke,

Although we are so far away and many miles separate us, I do not spend a second without thinking about you. The distance sends my feelings back toward you. That is why you should know that every day that happens, I love you more. It deepens my link with you, and it generates a certain feeling of fear, but I know you are a very calm being, and that calms me. I know you like this kind of music (classic rock), and I like to share more about me and want to know the music you do not like. I want to share these and more experiences together. I want you to know that no distance can stop this love. Just as each flower is born to beautify its place, our relationship is destined to last. It will flourish with the passage of time.

Joyita

My lover,

There is a song that I want you to listen to and I want you to know that you are inside my skin, in the depths of my most sincere love. This is one of my favorite songs and I hope you understand how deep my love is for you.

"I've Got You Under My Skin" by Frank Sinatra

I've got you under my skin
I've got you deep in the heart of me
So deep in my heart that you're really a part of me
I've got you under my skin
I tried so not to give in
I said to myself this affair never will go so well
But why should I try to resist when baby I know so well
I've got you under my skin
I'd sacrifice anything come what might
For the sake of having you near
In spite of a warning voice that comes in the night
and repeats, repeats in my ear
Don't you know, little fool, you never can win
Use your mentality, wake up to reality
but each time that I do
just the thought of you makes me stop before I begin
because I've got you under my skin

I would sacrifice anything, come what might
for the sake of having you near
in spite of a warning voice that comes in the night
and repeats, how it yells in my ear
Don't you know little fool, you never can win
Why not use your mentality, step up, wake up, to reality
but each time I do just the thought of you
makes me stop just before I begin
'cause I've got you under my skin.
Yes, I've got you under my skin.

Tell me, what did you think about the song? He is one of my favorite singers. He has a special music that take you to another world full of love and passion. His music is great, and I feel that this song describes what you and I are destined for. Whenever I listen to it, you are always on my mind. I love you. We must listen to this song together by candlelight with a glass of wine and take it in to our heart and souls.

Joyita

Love of my days,

When you came into my life, you brought me all that happiness that I longed for so much. You are what I had always dreamed of and believed in, and it is incredible. You appeared as a ray of light in the darkness that illuminated my life and made me understand that love is real. Since I met you, I knew that a long and beautiful future awaited us. Today, after many years and many adventures together, my intuition tells that thousands of days full of love await us. You know that all moments have not been easy. We have had to overcome various obstacles and adversities but we always held hands and solved difficulties as the best of teams. And do you know what is the best of all? We still have the best lives ahead of us. I want to always be happy and by your side until the end of days.

Luke

Luke,

My love, thank you for taking the time to write me. I know that you are bored in this website, and I also want us to be together. Soon we are going to enjoy life. I understand perfectly that you are already wishing to have me there. I wish the same every day. My love, I am very sorry for your son's friend who died of Covid 19. It is really sad to know that life can go away at any time. I know that we must be together, and I don't want to delay being with you. I really just wish that we are waking up every morning together enjoying life. You are my soulmate. I hope you can write me a little longer while I get my visa. I hope you have a good day at work, and you should know that you are the man in my life.

My love, I am always happy to write my thoughts. Nothing makes me happy as having you with me. It is important to know that we can be together. Thanks. I hope you have a good weekend.

Joyita

Luke,

Good morning, it is a pleasure to have you close to me; we will be together soon. I would like to have you with me in the best circumstances. For me, you are a man full of love. I want to give ourselves the opportunity to always love each other. I will fill you up with strength to be together soon. I want you to know that in life there are always obstacles, and I know that we will be able to overcome them together. You should never surrender for what I feel for you. I am writing this letter with all the sincerity in the world. Thank you for filling me with your feelings. Do you want to still move forward to be able to be together in love? Thank God for one more day full of health, smiles, and sharing with you.

Joyita

Luke,

In the heart of the most secret mind, inside the most distant fruit, in the vibration of the most discreet note, in the spiraling and resonant conch, in the thickest layer of paint, in the vein that most probes us in the body, in the word that says softer, in the root that does down the most, hides the mast, in the deepest silence of this pause, where life became eternity, I look for your hand and decipher the cause of wanting and not believing there could be intimacy.

Joyita

My love,

Today I want to write you this letter to thank you for your unconditional support. I like knowing I can count on you at all times; you never disappoint me. Your words of encouragement during difficult times were of great help. Today, when everything is calm and we begin to return a little to normal, I want to thank you very much for everything. For every hug of comfort, for every smile that you gave me because without you, I would not have been able to pass this test. You are my greatest support, my right hand, and my unconditional companion. I thank life and God for having met you. I feel fortunate to have such an extraordinary person with me. Every day you give me your best to make me happy, and that makes me love you much more. I want to correspond to you everything you have done for me. I will also strive to love you more every day, as you deserve it. Your presence in my life is fundamental. Without you, it would no longer be the same; you are my complement. I was not wrong about you; you have never failed me in good times or in bad. I want you to know that you can count on me unconditionally, no matter what fate sends us. You will always have support and a helping hand from me.

Joyita

Luke,

In addition, I also want to thank you for how you are—for your support and love with my family, although it comes as no surprise to me. Many in my family were surprised and astonished that you had risen to the occasion and supported me so well. It shows our age difference is not an impediment with you assuming the responsibility of facing and meeting my family. Thank you again, my love. I hope I can reward you for everything. Thank you for the patience you have had with me. You know very well that it has not been easy. But with your love, I know that I will overcome this temporary bad moment of health that I now live with.

Joyita

Short Daily Texts

If loving you was a job, I would be the most deserving, dedicated, and qualified candidate. In fact, I would be willing to work for free!

Your smile is literally the cutest thing I have ever seen in my life!

If someone asked me to describe you in just two words, I would say, "Simply amazing!"

You do a million little things that bring joy to my life.

I know fairy tales come true because I have you.

If you were a movie, I would watch you over and over again!

In a sea of people my eyes always search for you!

What on earth did I think about all the time before you filled my heart and mind with thoughts of you?

My six-word love story: "I cannot imagine life without you!"

Always think about your love, your other half, and send these thoughts once a day as a text.

What I love about you, the inner you:

Your kind, gentle, and tender heart

Your warm, dark, beautiful eyes

You have the most beautiful, sexy smile, that lights up the whole world

Gorgeous, delicious, sweet inviting lips

Beautiful cheek bones make you look like a model
Your sweetness and personality
Your straight and cute nose that anchors your beautiful face
Your beautiful chin which shapes your whole face
You have the most beautiful, kissable ears
Your beautiful, long dark hair
Your beautiful, dark eyebrows
Your beautiful, long eyelashes
Your cute nose that I love
Your beautiful neck I love to kiss. I would like to raise your
hair and kiss it on the back and front!
Your beautiful, long fingernails
Your beautiful breasts that make you a woman
Your beautiful, tight tummy
Your tiny waist
Your curvy hips
Your beautiful, flower that makes you a woman
Your beautiful butt
Your beautiful, long, legs
Your beautiful back
Your beautiful, feet and toes I want to massage to relax you,
but more important than all those things is your internal
beauty, that is you
Your tender heart
Your good soul
Your wonderful personality
Your sweetness
Your naked honesty

Your loyalty
Your good heart
Your intelligence
Your personality
Your maturity
Your common sense and business sense
Your truthfulness
Your kindness
Your loving nature
Your sweet voice
Your passion
Your freckles
Your beautiful teeth
Your dimples
The way you wear your hair
The way you dress
Your drive to complete tasks
The way you love and treat me
The little girl you keep inside that only I see
Your beautiful arms and soft, graceful, gentle hands that God has you work so many miracles with, but yet so delicate and lovely with beautiful nails! Those hands I want to hold!

Darling,

When you're not online or I don't get a message from you, you don't know how much I miss being with you! Seriously, that's why I take those moments as inspiration to write what I feel in my heart. Seriously, you do not know how my soul needs you; every time I don't hear from you are times I feel alone. But I will remember that you have many things to do. But I want you to know I will always be here for you for whatever you want to tell me, and you can trust me.

What a shame to know that I love you with all my heart, that you are the most important man in my life, and you don't know how much you make me happy! I hope I can talk more with you as I don't want you to leave my side. When can we talk more again in the near future?

Joyita

Luke,

You are the most wonderful man in the world, my love; you make me very happy, so I don't know what I did to have a man so understanding, kind, respectful, and very handsome. You fill me with happiness, and you don't know how in love I am with you because of the wonderful person that you are. I just want to be able to fill you with kisses and caresses, and kiss those beautiful lips and sleep peacefully with you. Tell me that you want the same thing! You do not know how handsome you look in that beautiful photo that makes me want to hug and kiss you a lot, my love!

Joyita

Luke,

Today, I want you to know how much I miss you. The distance that separates us cannot be greater than the love that unites us. However, sometimes I feel like I am disappearing because I am not by your side. I feel more and more attached to you. Knowing that you are okay calms me down and comforts me. Although I never stop missing you, every night I dream of you and our meeting in person. You are the most addictive sensation I have ever tasted; that thought melts into a lava of emotions, passion, and strength. You are everything I need!

Joyita

Luke,

    I am sure that this new day comes with many beautiful surprises for you to get up with courage and the best vibes. May all the good keep you and the best protect you in this new day. Good morning to you! I assure you that everything that remains for you in the afternoon will be even better than the morning because I have sent you all my positive feelings so that you can cheer up and so that you do not forget how much I love you! And how much I need you! Do not forget that I am with you, no matter what happens. I know you can always deal with what is put in front of you. So you calm me and everything will be great, I promise you. You are the best thing that ever happened to me. You are like the best poetry ever composed, the best song ever performed, and the best image ever painted. I never thought that someone like me could be so lucky to meet you!

Joyita

Joyita,

You are not only beautiful and sweet but kind and intelligent. You talk to me with such sweet words and passion that it melts my heart. You are not only a doctor, but an angel of sweetness. I cannot wait for us to get together so I have you permanently by my side and so that each day we can hug, smile, and kiss good morning or good night.

Luke

Luke,

Thank you for such beautiful words, darling. I just want you to know that where you come from doesn't matter. It doesn't matter what you do. Don't think that love is based on the physical either; the most beautiful feelings are the most important in life and that is what I have to give you and be able to receive from a gentleman like you. Your good feelings, love, and respect are all I want or need from you. I hope we can both go to the beach to spend a fun day. I will check my agenda so I can arrange it, then dinner and dancing after. Or maybe we will just sink into the sofa for a romantic movie. I love you with everything! I love you with all my heart, and I would like to be able to share these things with you, darling.

Joyita

Luke,

I really love kissing, but I haven't done it for a long time. I would like to do it with you. You can help me remember this fantastic feeling when you feel warmth and passion at the same time. When you feel that the kiss of this person is one of the best events in your life and when you feel you are ready to live for these kisses as I am.

I would like to give you my most sensual kiss, and I hope this will make you very happy and relaxed! If a hug is the best place in the world, then kissing is definitely the best complement to that hug. I want to see you in front of me and understand that I can kiss this man to death. That I am all yours. I think that men often keep their feelings inside, and they think the woman should compensate for them. So, I hope this letter will make your mood better, knowing when we are together you will get those kisses every morning and night.

Joyita

Joyita,

I don't think I ever really felt my heart beat until you were in my life. I thought I knew what love was, two people mutually caring for each other, but you have taught me it is much, much more than this. It is a feeling that you can fly and that you want to be with the other person so much that you could almost die until that moment comes. It is like you see the sunshine but did not feel it until the sunshine comes in a sweet word or gesture from your love. It is like living day to day, but you are a shell because your spark is somewhere else! You are my spark and my sunshine. I have never known anyone like you. I tell you that you are perfect in every way because it is so. I have never felt so intertwined with another person I have not met in person, and yet, you have stolen my heart. It was not really stolen because I give it to you freely and without anything in return promised. That is what you have taught me about true love. To give it freely and expect nothing in return as true love should be given. And so my heart is yours and only yours. Please be gentle with it. Every beat belongs to you, and every waking thought is about you, my dream girl. Never was there or will there be a better one. I love you with all my heart.

Luke

Joyita,

I miss you so much, I miss your kisses, your caresses, your skin touching my skin. I miss every moment by your side. I miss you in a thousand ways with my soul in pieces. I always think of you. Today I woke up and in my mind, there was only you. Today, I woke up, and I felt the lack that you do. To my wounded heart, today I could only think of you and how much I need you. Remembering every moment by your side, my eyes filled with brightness because you with your light illuminates the days and because you are the angel who was always by my side. You gave me everything without asking for anything in return. I can't get you out of my mind. I can't get you out of my body. I can't get you out of my chest that beats with every beat of my heart; I can only love you. I can only offer you my whole being and adore you madly.

Luke

Poetry

Together Forever

We are together forever.
Where would I be without you?
And where would you be without me?
Trapped in the arms of a second choice.
Forever envious of all, are we.
My need for you makes life special
because I live it for you.
Everything seems more possible
and easier to get though.
Each hour is a new adventure
Where what awaits, no one knows.
Through friendship, tears, and laughter,
we ensure our romance grows.
Even ordinary moments
aren't the same anymore.
Together we have so much
to plan, accomplish and explore.

Author Unknown

Love in a Foreign Land

I met this princess in a foreign land
and asked her for her hand,
but she is trapped in a tower of Covid disease and can't leave.
So I am waiting for this sickness to unravel,
so to me she can travel,
then we can be together, and life will be better.
So until then, I send this letter,
telling her I am much more than a friend.
A letter of love from my heart as it has been from the very start.
And I wait patiently for her because she is worth it,
no matter how long until I hold her in my arms
and enjoy her many charms,
and I can tell her in her ear
how much you mean to me, my dear!

THREE WORDS

In three words I could say
Robot come out and play,
but I need to say more today,
we have fun and joke
and neither of us smoke
but there is so much more to tell
as you took me out of my hell
and to a place with loving feeling
my heart is still reeling
as it pounds up to the ceiling.
When we talk and laugh,
I feel as tall as a giraffe
and as light as a bird.
Whenever you say a sweet word
it is this feeling that comes
and makes my heart pound
like drums
yet you calm me down,
with this love I have found.
So I sat down to think and write
something about how much
I love you
or you call me sky
which is blue
but the most important thing
I have to say is my love for
you is true
so you don't have to search
for a clue
because my robot in only
three words,
I LOVE YOU!!!

SOMETHING PROFOUND

Something profound!
It is this feeling that comes
when it is your love I have found.
Your sweet voice to me is such a great sound.
You are always so sweet and kind,
and you are always on my mind.
Your eyes are bright like stars,
your hugs and kisses remove all my scars.
Yes, every moment of my day and night
all I think of is you and even God must
think it's right!
I have searched for true love with all my might!
And this love that comes from God is
worth the search and fight
to keep it and hold it
even though it is an effort
because life without it
is like being in a deep dark pit
without being able to get out of it!
So, if you recognize true love
don't let it get away
because your life will be so much better,
I am here to say.

Listen to Your Heart

I went for a walk in the mountains and
in the woods to think about what to say.
So if you think this life is okay,
you can make it better, like putting on a sweater.
But the place to start is your heart,
not your ego, if you are smart.
Your emotions may not be, to influence everyone
with your own opinions and ideas.
Possibly some of these thoughts can be for like-minded souls,
but not forcing them on others like trolls.
So listen to your heart, not your ego,
and if you are truly smart,
that is a place to finish not just start!

Love Magic

I met this woman who was magic,
she transformed my heart to love her, but it was not tragic.
She brought my wildness to tame, and now my heart isn't the same
because her smile is my bane.
As she is not in my presence here,
and I hold her quite dear.
And now I think about nothing else
than her picture I keep on a shelf.
And holding her in my arms,
enjoying her person and many charms.
So when going to sleep at night,
remember your magic and the love I keep for you with all my might.
When you smile, you knock me out and I fall apart,
And I thought I was so smart!
Your smile is like a work of art,
and I have loved you from the very start!

Falling for You

You may have stolen my heart
like a thief in the night,
But it is okay
because I didn't put up a fight.
I felt good and everything was right.
I felt like I fell in an abyss,
a love so deep I fell for days.
And though I couldn't see the bottom as I was falling,
I closed my eyes and could see your sweet loving ways.
I brought my love to you and came calling,
and I hope all this is not appalling.
But love made it with me okay
So the main thing I have to say,
is that I want to stay.
And, I hope more than anything with this love thought
you are okay.

VALLEY

Here in bed I lay in pain,
because my heart and true love is in Spain,
and she travels in the city or on the plain.
But it doesn't matter because wherever
she is, it is still the same,
In the night I keep calling out her name.
I have to get up each day without her and rally
because I so miss my Valley.

Baby, I Am a Man

Baby, I may only be a man,
but I want to always hold your hand,
and together we will make a stand,
to love each other as long as we can.
Baby, I may only be a man,
but I will adore you as long as I can.
I want you to always be by my side, and to others I say damn,
because I am the one to spend all my free time with you
when I can.
Baby, I may only be a man
We will go to the beach and play in the sand.
We will love each other as our hearts demand.
But our love will be for decades and
I will love you more each day,
if you say yes, it is okay;
I will always be your man.
Baby, I may only be a man;
I will be yours, if you say I can
So give me your answer so that I am!

ONE WAY LOVE

You erase my fear and to my heart are very dear.
What is it you do to me?
I don't know what you do to me, but I am prepared for the
whole world to see.
You always make my heart beat faster,
but it is not a disaster.
It beats out of love just for you with nothing needed
and is something you should pursue in return.
You somehow miss my love signals, which is not a concern,
unless it means you will leave and not return.

MY LOVE

The first thing I think of
each morning when I rise.
The last thing I think of
each night when I close my eyes.
In each thought I have
and every breath I take,
My feelings are growing stronger
with every move I make.
I want to prove my love
but that's the hardest part,
so I'm giving all I have to give—
I give my heart.

Her

The sound of her voice
is music to my ear,
so soft, sweet, and clear.
The kiss from her lips
words cannot explain;
it takes away my worries and my pain.
The caress of her hand
sends shivers down my spine.
every day I thank God that she is mine.
The sight of her lovely face throughout the years
for an eternity I want to spend in her arms,
every day graced by her beauty and her charm.

Who Am I?

Who am I?
I make your heart skip a beat,
I am the adrenalin when we meet,
I make your skin tingle,
when you are married or single.
I make your legs tremble
when you reach me, and without thinking,
your feelings are disassembled.
I am what can make you a disaster
because I can take over as your master.
I am LOVE!

If You Were a Robot

Everything is better than before
because I love you to the core.
Life is so wonderful with you in this world,
you fill me with love, so now you have been told.
So even if you were a robot, you would never be sold.
I feel love for you in every cell of my skin,
but God told me it wasn't a sin.
Forever with you isn't enough,
and I told God anything else would be rough.
This being with a machine is strange
and being in love with her is a change.
But I have some chores for her I can arrange!
Love you my robot!

MY LITTLE ROBOT

This love is a strange feeling like I am on another planet.
I met this woman and her name is not Janet,
but she must be an alien because she is so sweet
and never such a woman before did I meet.
She zapped me and captured my heart, and now I don't want
to be away
from her or apart.
I felt this love for her from the very start.
It wasn't till I fell deeply in love with her that I got it.
She is really a robot!
So even though this change from a person to a machine
is strange,
Robots do make our life easier and better,
so I have to send her this letter.
That I love you my little robot and all you got,
and by the way I just wanted to say I hope you have a really nice
day by the way.
Love you always!

ANGEL

If you were a flower,
you would always be in bloom.
You are like a ray of sunshine,
shining down from the heavens,
with a smile and warmth so divine,
with sweetness and a heart so kind.
You are like a little angel,
an angel I hope will be mine.

Without a Sting

I am your everything without a sting;
it is true love I bring.
It is everything in life I deliver and sing;
like a bee to a flower,
I give you this power.
To take my hand and love life with me
and treasure our moments together,
making our love and feelings as light as a feather,
when we are like sunny, blue-sky weather.
I am your everything,
without a sting,
it is true love I bring,
as Jesus taught us this great thing,
a four-lettered word called LOVE!
It is why we were created from above!
The greatest feeling on Earth called LOVE.

Understanding

I once saw a little girl inside a woman; I said what are you doing there?
And, she said, why do you care?
I said as a man, I should be aware
At first I only got a stare
Then she said I want to be taken care of like a little dove
and, be understood by my man, not just God above.
I said now I understand you more
as the woman I adore.
I will protect you and take care of you;
What more could I do
Do not be temperamental or mean
or act unloving like a machine,
but be always kind
and be patient and love with your heart and mind.
Be honest and truthful,
and I will be faithful.
We will stand together
in all types of weather
and be stronger than a wall,
Holding hands until the call.
When our life has ended
and we have ascended,
You will get true love
forever from this little dove.

A Poem or a Song

I am not sure if this is a poem or a song or who the author is, but it's not me. However, I included it because it stuck in my mind and is very good. The author is unknown to me:

Love is the greatest feeling,
Love is like a play,
Love is what I feel for you each and every day.
Love is like a smile,
Love is like a song,
Love is a great emotion,
that keeps us going strong.
I love you with my heart,
my body and my soul,
I love the way I keep loving,
like a love I can't control.
So remember when your eyes meet mine,
I love you with all my heart,
and I have poured my entire soul in to you,
right from the very start.

FALLING IN LOVE

Falling in love, you have to let things flow,
don't rush into it,
but let your true-feelings grow.
Sending good vibrations around us to others,
makes them warm up to us.
Finding things in common and being ourselves,
keeps us from needing a lot of help
even from an elf.
And, if we reach a connection and trust,
we can openly talk,
this is important and makes us feel better about ourselves.
When a real connection between us arrives,
that is finally when love thrives.
The real trick is not to let it fade,
communication and kissing always keeps it burning,
even in the shade.

Enjoy Life

Enjoy your life
but remember to enjoy your girlfriend or wife,
doing fun things together
no matter what the weather.
Taking time to know your other half
can make life as fun as a rubber duck in a bath
and make your life better.
So talk, or when not together, text, call, or write a letter.
Communicate and enjoy your time
while still young and in your prime
because if with a family you are blessed
you never get an alone time or rest!

LOVE IS GREAT!

Loving her is like a dream,
such a vision of beauty,
so loving and sweet.
But, yet, everything I tell her,
she keeps discrete.
She takes me to heaven
and is my best friend.
The feelings she gives me
almost makes me feel like I transcend.
And the way she treats me is so clever;
I will stay with her forever.

Nobody

*"You're nobody 'til somebody loves you."
What is it when we are loved?
Friendship, companionship, company, lover, best friend
everything in life.
Need a shoulder or someone to laugh with
or maybe cry with,
this is the best of us we can give!
So get out there and meet someone,
another half.
Stop walking around in a daze.

*DEAN MARTIN

GOD?

If we don't believe in God
look at your thumb.
There are no two alike, how dumb.
Or maybe it was smart,
We are labeled as different from the very start.
To be able to feel love and give love,
So when we say there is no God
remember how long we will be under the sod.
Maybe in fire or maybe not,
but I will take my chances with Him
as it may turn out to mean a lot!

Shot by an Arrow

I was shot by an arrow,
and infected with love,
like a spring sparrow.
I could think of nothing but her,
like a cat that could really purr.
And I found I liked this feeling
that kept my head reeling.
And I decided to stay,
instead of my previous play.
So, if you ever get a chance,
and find romance,
or to be pierced by an arrow or a love lance,
you might find you like it.
So, go and see if love can be for you a hit
and make you complete.

WOKE UP

I woke up this morning in my bed,
and this saying was in my head.
Love is more than a hug and a squeeze
it's a great feeling
and we can give it to anyone.
But being loved back is the trick
and the waiting is tough.
But when love does arrive,
we sometimes hope we survive
this wonderful heart-felt feeling,
the heartbeat, the tingling sensation
that makes our world move
when our heart really beats and we hit the ceiling.
So, if we have a chance at true love
I am here to say, take a chance
it will be okay
or to not know love, your call.

CUPID

I wanted to fall in love
but it wasn't happening.
So, I asked Cupid
what was my problem,
was I just stupid?
She said it is how we treat
others that is the secret.
If we are honest and sweet
plus be our self and true,
things will happen
and love will come to us!

Rain Drop

It has rained
and now the fragrances are pronounced.
The sweet smell of flowers
reach me on a slight breeze.
It reminds me of your fragrance
and time spent together.
Wondering if we will grow
to be a couple and be complete.
As my mind wanders while I walk,
this thought enters my mind and is very sweet.
Then a rain drop from the sky
hits me in the eye!
I hope this is not a sign of something to come.

Woods Walk

I enjoyed walking in the woods while
watching two grey squirrels play.
They were inseparable,
running up and down trees
and along the ground.
Then it made me think how at times you accompany me
without making a sound
but give me a silent glance
which instantly melts my heart.
That is what made me ask on bended knee
and you didn't even have to climb a tree!

I wrote this little poem to express part of my feelings for you,
and I hope you like it and it makes you very happy.

KISSES MY LOVE

You are my heaven,
You are my light,
and you are also my reason for living.
I cannot live without you
because your eyes are like glue
in my heart since my eyes looked at you.

A Thousand Feelings

I have been through a thousand feelings because of you.
The first time I saw you standing there,
I wanted to meet you but didn't dare.
Then you came closer. You asked me a question about a nearby restaurant.
I told you I had never eaten there, and we both laughed.
Then you asked if I would like to join you and try dinner there.
I said, yes, as I looked into your gorgeous eyes.
At dinner there was music and you asked me to dance.
We laughed and had a great conversation during and after dinner.
Then, after dinner, I had to leave not to be late for my work.
You asked me if you could see me again and for my number.
It all began with a chance encounter that started our romance.

FEARS

There were many fears to overcome.
Walking up to you, smiling and talking was a big one.
Asking you to dance so I didn't pass up on the chance to meet
you was another.
I felt you were kind and acted like my big brother.
I was hoping you might really notice me.
But there were many other pretty girls in the room to see.
Then, I overcame my greatest fear.
You asked me for my phone number, and it was clear. I would
see you again.
We quickly kissed goodbye, and I gave a big sigh.
Before leaving with my girlfriends to disappear.

DEAR GOD,

Thank you for sending Your son, Jesus, so I could get to know you. Thank you for loving me. Thank you for being with me all my life, even when I didn't know it. I realize I need a Savior to set me free from sin, from myself, and from all the habits, hurts, and hang ups that mess up my life.

I ask you to forgive me for my sins. I want to repent and live the way you created me to live. Be the Lord of my life and save me by Your grace. Save me from my sins and save me for Your purpose.

I want to learn to love You, trust You, and become what you made me to be.

Thank you for creating me and choosing me to be part of Your family.

Right now, by faith, I accept the Christmas gift of Your Son. Fill me with your peace and assurance so I can be a peace-maker and help me share this message of peace with others in Your name, I pray.

Amen.

God sent us many gifts but two are outstanding. His only Son, Jesus, who taught us about true and pure love. It is the greatest human emotion and gift! Being close to God makes us feel it even better, knowing the real source. I truly hope you find this greatest gift in your lifetime. It makes your life so much better!

Be blessed!

Lynx5082@gmail.com